I0757375

This Belongs to

Dandie Dinmont Terrier

Pembroke Welsh Corgi

Golden Retriever

French Bulldog

Chow Chow

Bullmastiff

Pharaoh Hound

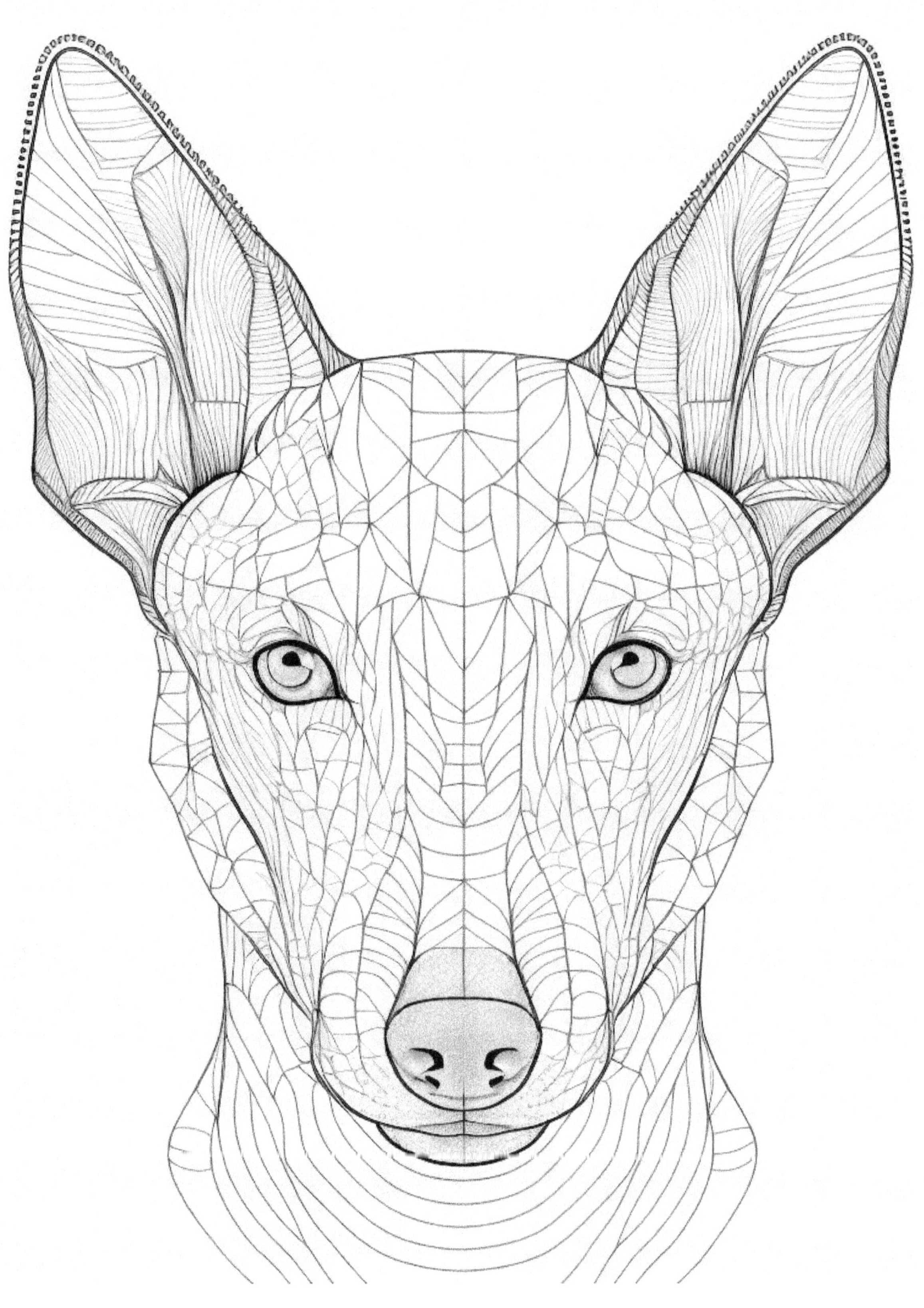

Greater Swiss Mountain Dog

Belgian Malinois

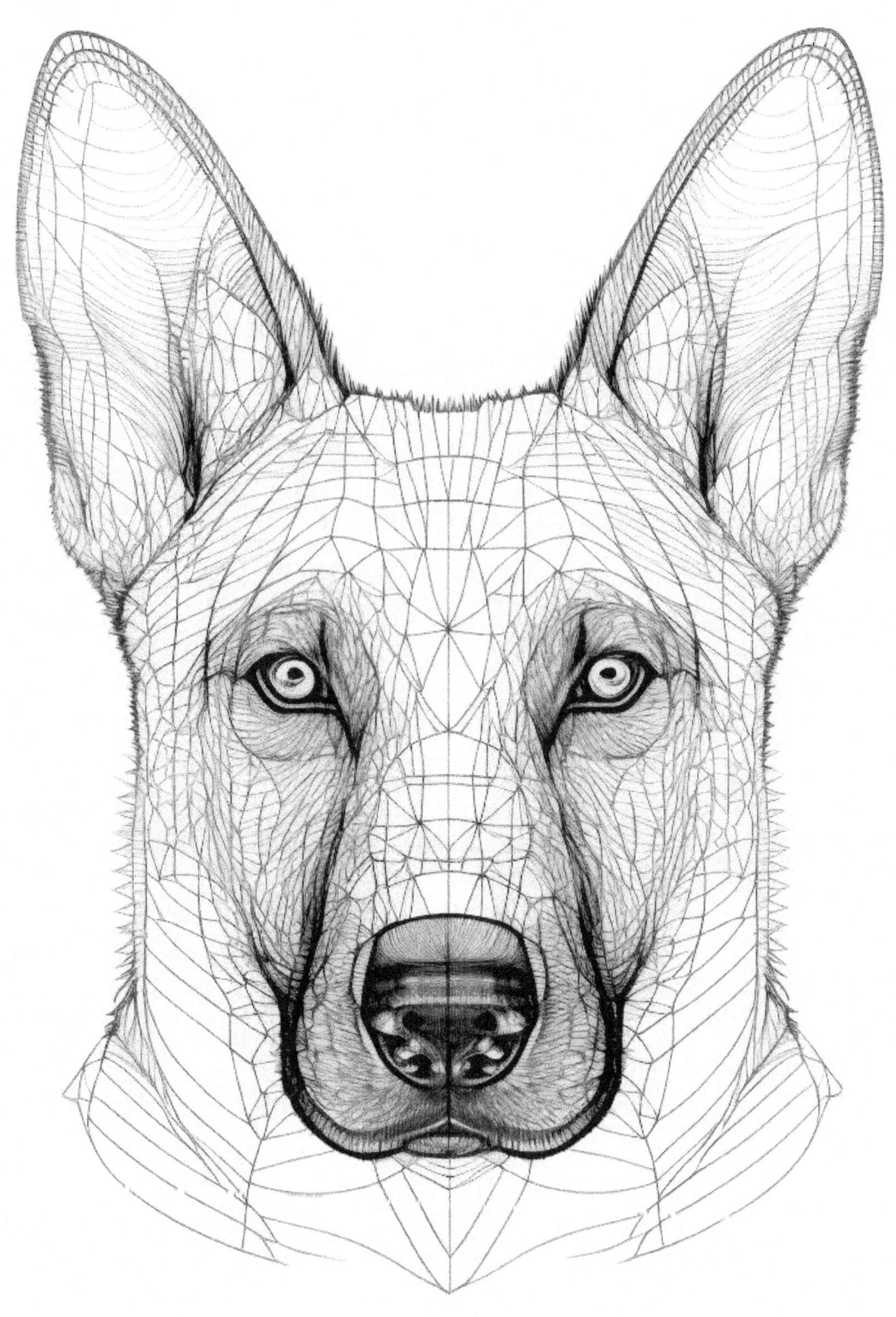

Dogue de Bordeaux

Irish Setter

Irish Wolfhound

Mastiff

German Shorthaired Pointer

Australian Terrier

Glen of Imaal Terrier

Belgian Tervuren

Australian Cattle Dog

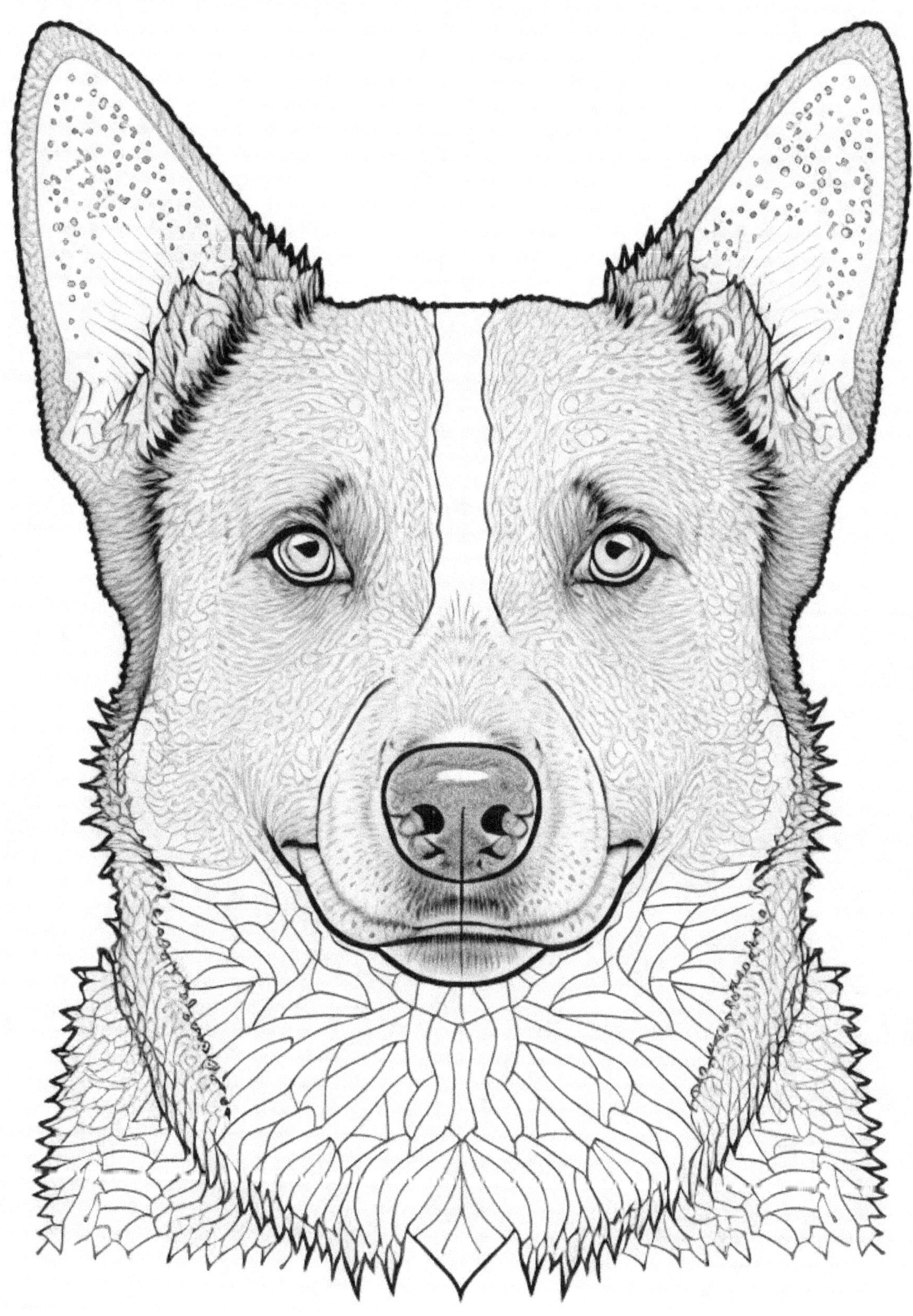

Maltese

American Foxhound

Canaan Dog

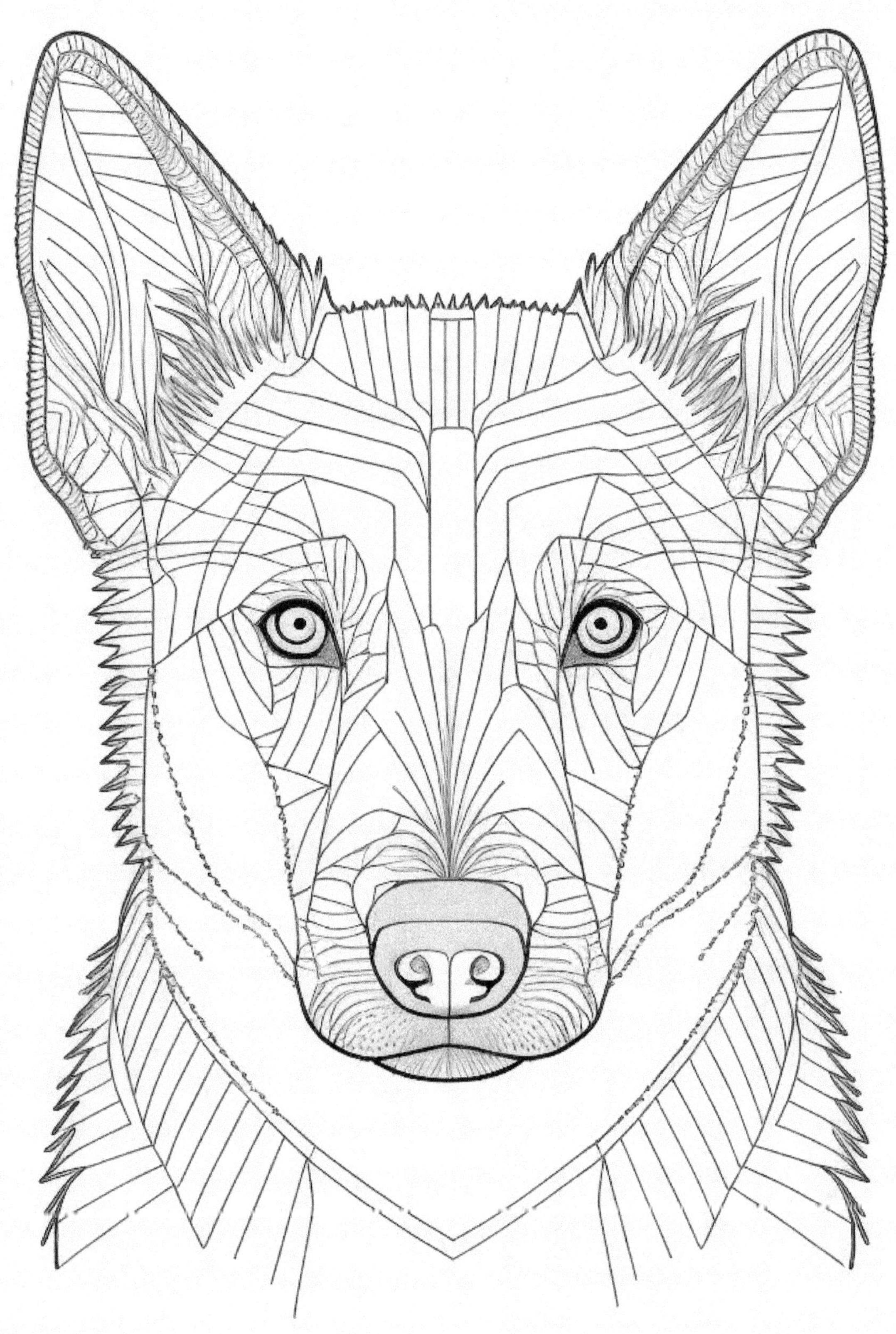

English Setter

Old English Sheepdog

Icelandic Sheepdog

Norwegian Elkhound

Chinese Crested

Lhasa Apso